M ALE,
M ACHO
&M AGNIFICENT

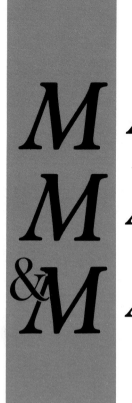

MALE, MACHO & MAGNIFICENT

Compiled by June Couch

COLUMBUS BOOKS
LONDON

First published in Great Britain in 1986 by
Columbus Books, Devonshire House,
29 Elmfield Road, Bromley, Kent BR1 1LT

Designed by Kirby-Sessions, London

Printed in Italy

ISBN 0 86287 184 0

CONTENTS

'Men have become peacocks again.'

Gavin Robinson, Gavin's Models

Why does a man become a model? How many young boys express the wish to grace a catwalk or face the searching gaze of a photographer's lens when they grow up?

There can't be many – yet among the girls it is a different story. We know the names of the top women models – Marie Helvin, Jerry Hall, Cheryl Tiegs – but how many of us could name a single *male* model?

Yet if we look around us, we will notice that the male image is everywhere, selling us not only clothes but cars, sports equipment, booze, aftershave, cigarettes, shower gel and services . . . little did Sir John Millais know what he was starting when he allowed his painting of a beautiful tousle-haired boy blowing bubbles to be used as a soap manufacturer's brand image.

The women may still outnumber the men, but the men are coming on strong. Both Roger Moore and Sean Connery have been models, and they are by no means the only ones. Ten years ago, only four of London's top model agencies could offer men. Now many more do, and some have as many as fifty or sixty names on their books. Given the face and the physique, a man can go a long way as a model. What other legitimate occupation pays so well for so little – if 'little' can describe what a successful model has to offer?

Of course, nature has done its part: the features are regular, the skin is clear and the body is beautiful . . . Height is important – 6 foot or slightly over is fairly standard – and weight should be in proportion. Even if the model appears to be in trim, he needs to be able to smile without looking pudgy, which may mean keeping below his usual weight. He must look good from all angles, too – legs and torso, of course, but bookers may also want to see that the back of his head looks good too. Today's professional on the modelling circuit probably works pretty hard at keeping himself up to scratch. He will almost certainly exercise and watch his diet – which is not to say he spends hours in a gym every day and follows a strict diet; none the less, he knows he cannot let himself run to seed, overdoing the late nights and the booze. If he is in fact a sports fanatic, he must keep his enthusiasm in check – too much muscle and he will no longer be a stock size, and that will lose him work.

He must ensure that he is always properly equipped for a shoot, with clean shirts and at least two immaculate pairs of shoes, one black, one brown, which are never worn except for modelling. And he must be punctual: photographers' time is an expensive commodity. What most models like most about the business is its variety – no two jobs are the same, and location work can make up for quite a lot of less interesting stints in a studio. If they are working for a top couturier they may only be there as a dinner-jacketed foil to the dazzingly gowned female models, but more and more nowadays the men are needed to promote 'young' fashions – which can demand considerable physical exertion on the catwalk. Rehearsing for a show recently, the boys were going through a repertoire of forward rolls, back flips, 'grinding' and body popping to show off thermal underwear. For them, it was all in a day's work.

'Men are more interested in clothes, and the clothes around now are more interesting.'

Neville Gates, Nev's

'It either all fits or it doesn't.'

Laraine Ashton

What else? Only an indefinable something which makes a face relate to a camera lens, perhaps a flair for wearing clothes, rather than letting clothes wear him . . . With some clothes it is easy, but the man who can make a cheap polyester suit from a chainstore look like a million dollars in a mail-order catalogue is the one who is really worth his fee.

He must be versatile, too, adept at transforming his appearance from beach-boy to business executive to disco kid as required, whatever the image required. So he'll know exactly how to style his hair and how to handle cosmetics.

All this, and several bucketfuls of luck, especially 'being in the right place at the right time', go to make a top model, and though the working life of a male model is longer than that of his female counterpart, he will probably have to think ahead to what happens afterwards, when the bookings cease to flow in, right from the beginning. Acting attracts quite a few, and certainly they will have acquired one great asset – to be able to react unselfconsciously and on cue to the camera. Others see the money they have earned as models as being just the first step, something that will become the foundation for a second career.

Male, Macho and Magnificent presents twenty-one top male models from Britain, America, Australia and northern Europe, and gives them the opportunity to reveal something of the man behind the image – their hopes and ambitions, their tastes in clothes, music, films, literature, places they like to go, and, of course, what they think about the business in which they make their living. Some reveal how they got started, others their plans for the future. Then there are the pictures – a portfolio for each model that gives some idea of the versatility and sheer photogenic presence that have put each model at the top of his profession.

9

*C*HRIS
*C*ONNOLLY

A Welshman from Port Talbot, Chris Connolly was obliged to play rugby at school but was spotted playing club football on Saturdays. At 14 he played in England, Ireland and Scotland for the Welsh Schoolboys team, then worked up to the Youth International team. He has a full Equity card and has had small parts in television programmes such as Dr Who, Big Deal, Juliet Bravo, Oscar Wilde *and* Top of the Pops.

Sport: I started off with Hereford United at 16, then I transferred to Nottingham Forest in the 1st Division. I thought it would be a good career move but I hated every minute of it and couldn't settle down at the club so I transferred to Sweden to play for Kalmar, which is about 50 miles from Malmo.

Sweden: I loved Sweden – it's the most beautiful country in the world. Not only did I enjoy the football there, I enjoyed living in Sweden very much – everything is so clean, the people are friendly and the standard of living is very high. My mother is Swedish so I lived with relatives over there – and of course, most Swedes speak good English.

Modelling: I was seen playing football and asked if I'd like to be a model. I said no, I wasn't interested – and then I broke my leg playing football in Sweden. I'd had three years as a player and wasn't interested in staying in football as a trainer or a manager, so I ended up modelling. I'm enjoying modelling at the moment and don't regret not being able to play football professionally.

Home: At the moment I'm living in the YMCA in Tottenham Court Road. It's marvellous – there's everything there for me. I love to train every day and there are swimming-pool facilities, weight-lifting, athletics . . .

Acting: I really enjoy acting. My ambition is to be a professional actor and break into films.

No regrets about pro football . . .

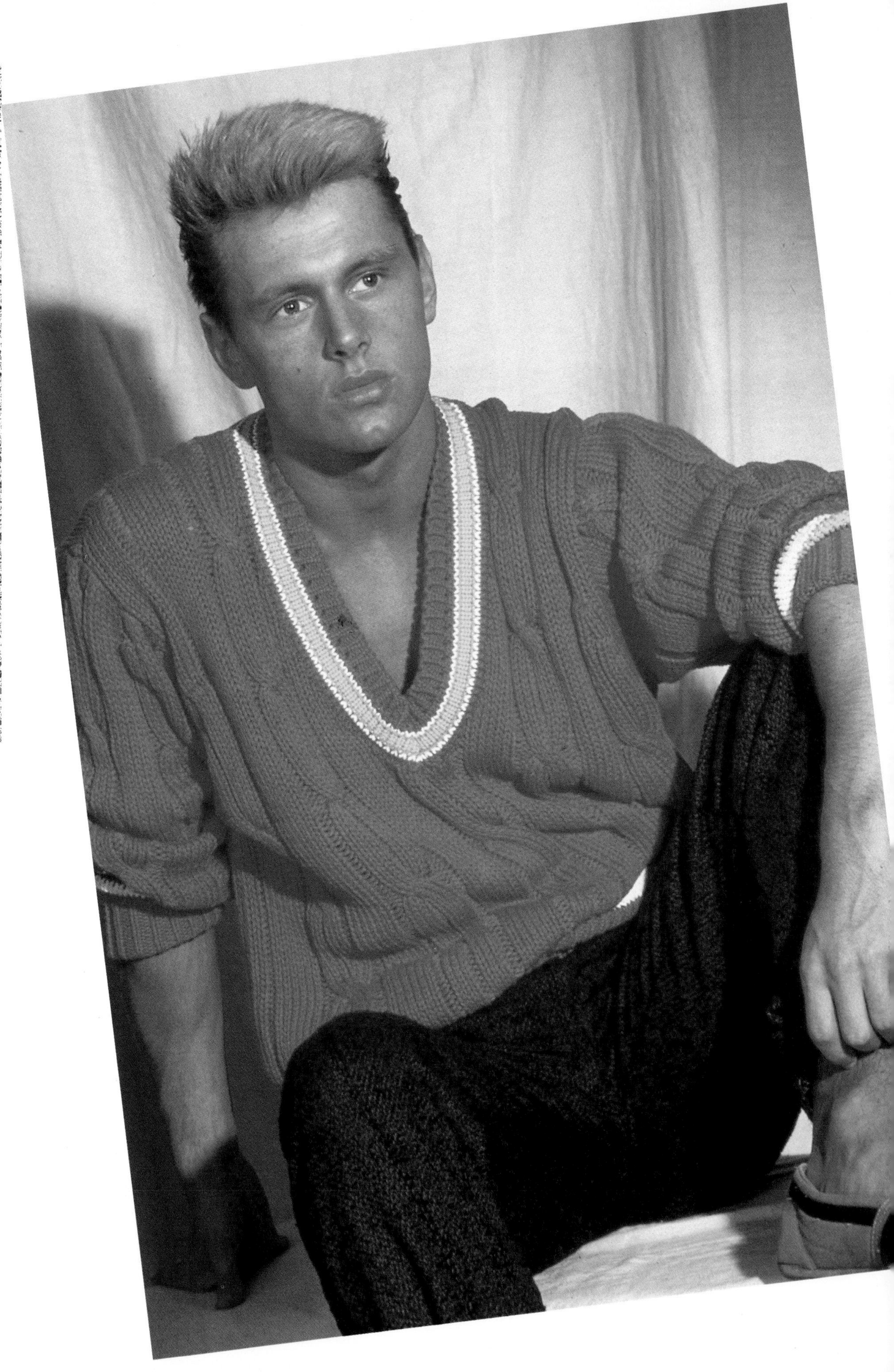

CHRIS CONNOLLY

Birthdate: 12 December 1964
Height: 5′11½″ (1.82m)
Hair: Blond
Star sign: Sagittarius
Weight: 12½ stones (175lb/79.38kg)
Eyes: Green

Personal favourites
Time of day: 8pm
Town: Hereford
Car: Porsche
Colour: Blue
Food: Sunday dinner
Drink: Orange juice
Hobbies: Keep-fit; cinema
Film: *Stir Crazy*
Actor/actress: Jerry Lewis; Raquel Welch
Book: *The Secret Diary of Adrian Mole Aged 13¾* (Sue Townsend)
Magazine: Sports magazines
TV show: *Soap*
Hero/heroine: George Best
Cartoon: Tom & Jerry
Music: Motown
Musician/group: Culture Club; Diana Ross
Places to go: Sweden
Holiday spots: Greece
Sport: Football
Sportsman/woman: Steve Ovett
Animal/pet: My cat
Ambitions/goals: To act in films
Clothing store: Toro
Aftershave lotion: Aramis
Fantasy: Playing in the F.A. Cup Final
Fear: Not being able to train
Agency: Gavin's Models

*H*OWARD *D*ENNIS

*H*oward Dennis's parents are from Trinidad but he has never been there. He is a born and bred Londoner.

Modelling: I left school with no idea what I wanted to do. I worked for an interior design company, which I hated, then for a clothing company. A friend then suggested I should try modelling and I got accepted by an agency. It certainly wasn't anything the careers master at school had suggested. I enjoy modelling now, but to begin with it was very difficult. Looked at from the outside it seems like an easy occupation because people just see the end result – a nice picture or commercial – but actually getting there, the wind-up of yourself, the selling aspect of yourself, that's the hard part.

Travel: Travelling is one of the perks of the job. I spent a year in Australia, which I loved – the way of life, the climate, the people, the space, the surf. There seem to be so many opportunities in Australia – I was offered lots of different jobs nothing to do with modelling, which wouldn't happen in Britain.

South Africa: The first job I got was a week's shoot in South Africa. This was very strange for me. Apartheid does exist – it's grim and you can't ignore it

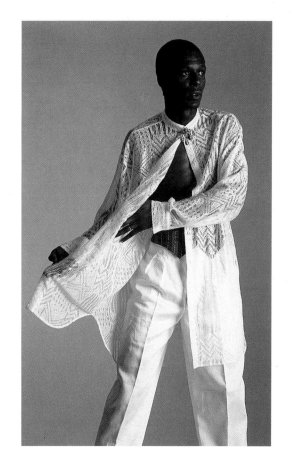

People just see the end result –
a nice picture or commercial –
but actually getting there,
the wind-up of yourself,
the selling aspect of yourself,
that's the hard part.

– but I met some good people, both black and white, and the country is magnificent.

The future: If I wasn't modelling I'd like to be a documentary photographer, but men model for longer than women so I'll be around a bit longer yet. With male modelling you're actually increasing your work output over the years, whereas with girls you reach a peak and that's the end. My girlfriend is a model and at 21 she's having to compete with girls of 15 and 16. You can't do that for long.

Keeping fit: I keep fit generally by cycling, walking and swimming.

Food: I eat enormous amounts of food. There's no strict diet – so long as I eat things that are good for me – and I never eat trash food. I'm a brilliant cook!

19

HOWARD DENNIS

Birthdate: 13 July 1960
Height: 6'2" (1.88m)
Hair: Black
Star sign: Cancer
Weight: 12 stones (168lb/ 76.2kg)
Eyes: Brown

Personal favourites
Time of day: Midnight
Town: Sydney
Car: Ferrari
Colour: Red
Food: West Indian
Drink: Beer
Hobbies: Photography; cycling; dancing; frisbee
Film: *The Jungle Book*
Actor/actress: Jack Nicholson; Katharine Hepburn
Book: *Oxford English Dictionary*
Author: Marguerite Yourcenar
Magazine: *National Geographic*
TV show: *Spitting Image*
Hero/heroine: Sydney Poitier; Boadicea
Cartoon: Donald Duck
Music: Reggae; soul; blues
Musician/group: Bob Marley; Sade; Mozart; Stevie Wonder
Places to go: China; Great Barrier Reef; Egypt
Holiday spots: Trinidad and Rio (both for the carnival)
Sport: Surfing; tennis
Sportsman/woman: Ed Moses; Nadia Comaneci
Ambitions/goals: To be successful and happy
Clothing store: Woodhouse
Clothing designer: Armani; Charlie Allen
Aftershave lotion: Halston
Fantasy: Having blue eyes
Fear: Being unhappy
Agency: Nev's

R USS
B OEHM

*R*uss *Boehm came originally from California but while living in London he became engaged to Christine, a Greek girl from Athens, who has lived in London for twelve years. They plan a Catholic wedding in London followed by a honeymoon in St Lucia.*

Travel: Christine is an air hostess for British Airways so when we marry we shall be eligible for concessions on flights. We'll never again have such a good opportunity to travel so we're planning a trip abroad every day off we have. I hope to see most of Europe very soon, though I have already modelled in Portugal and Israel. I've also visited many parts of Britain as I've gone with Christine when she has been working on internal flights.

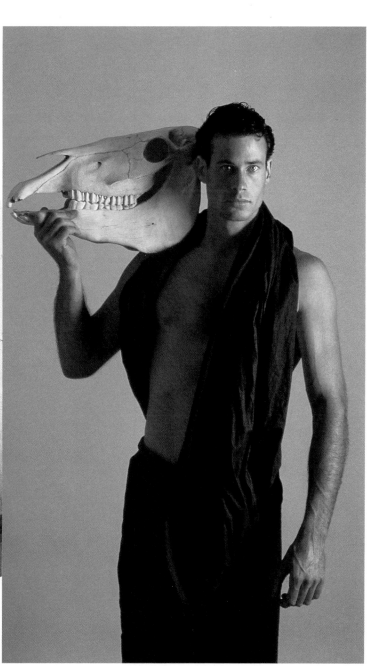

My favourite sport used to be motocross,
but you can't model on crutches.

Other jobs: I enjoy modelling but I am also a qualified electrician and work as a partner with my father in an electrical contracting firm. This takes the pressure off a bit when I go to a casting as one job supplements the other.

Sports: I like a lot of sport but I spend most of my free time playing golf. My favourite sport used to be motocross, but I smashed my legs twice and had to give it up – you can't model on crutches. I've played quite a bit of soccer in England and been in training with a local team in Gunnersbury Park [Ealing, West London]. It's very different from American football, but I'm trying hard to get into one of their bottom teams!

Spare time: Christine and I like the night-life in London. We go to the clubs, but I usually get told off when I take over the whole floor with my wild dance style.

RUSS BOEHM

Birthdate: 16 March 1959
Height: 6′2″ (1.88m)
Hair: Dark brown
Star sign: Pisces
Weight: 12 stones 2lb
  (170lb/77.11kg)
Eyes: Green

Personal favourites
Time of day: 10pm in
  summer
Town: San Francisco
Car: Porsche 911 SC
Colour: Dark blue
Food: Pasta
Drink: Any tropical rum
  drink
Hobbies: All sports,
  especially dirt bikes
Film: *Altered States*
Actor/actress: Clint
  Eastwood; Jill Clayburgh
Book: *Lucifer's Hammer*
  (Larry Niven and Jerry
  Pournelle)
Author: Robert Ludlum
Magazine: *Life*
TV show: *Magnum*
Cartoon: *Superman*; *Cat
  Woman*; *The Flintstones*
Music: Rock; jazz
Musician/group: Police;
  Phil Collins; Kenny
  Loggins
Places to go: Any sandy
  beach
Holiday spots: Baja
  California
Sport: Motocross
Sportsman/woman:
  Emlyn Hughes
Ambitions/goals: To work
  all over the world; to be
  the best at anything
Clothing store: Next
Agency: Models One

*E*DWARD
*H*EMPEL

*B*orn in London and educated at Millfield, Edward Hempel claims to have received his 'further education' by working around the world.

Early career: I went to Egypt for four months and worked on a site in Cairo building a hotel. Then I joined up with a friend and we ended up in Australia. We spent about two years there and came back through Asia. My girlfriend joined us for some of the time and we had a cat travelling with us too. We set up various little businesses in Australia swindling the Australians! We had a firewood business, buying chippings from a wood cutting factory 30 or 40 miles out of Sydney, trucked it down in a lorry and then had the Boy Scouts bagging them up at 50 cents a bag. We sold the bags at 5 bucks. Then we went up to Queensland. We were in Cairns, down to 50 bucks between us, when the annual fair came to town. We saw these photographers taking pictures and giving people a card to pick up the prints the next week in a local shop. We went one better and spent our last 50 bucks on a Polaroid camera . . . and cleaned up. Back in London, I got a job with an estate agent and learnt about property. Still short of cash, I took up a friend's suggestion and went into modelling.

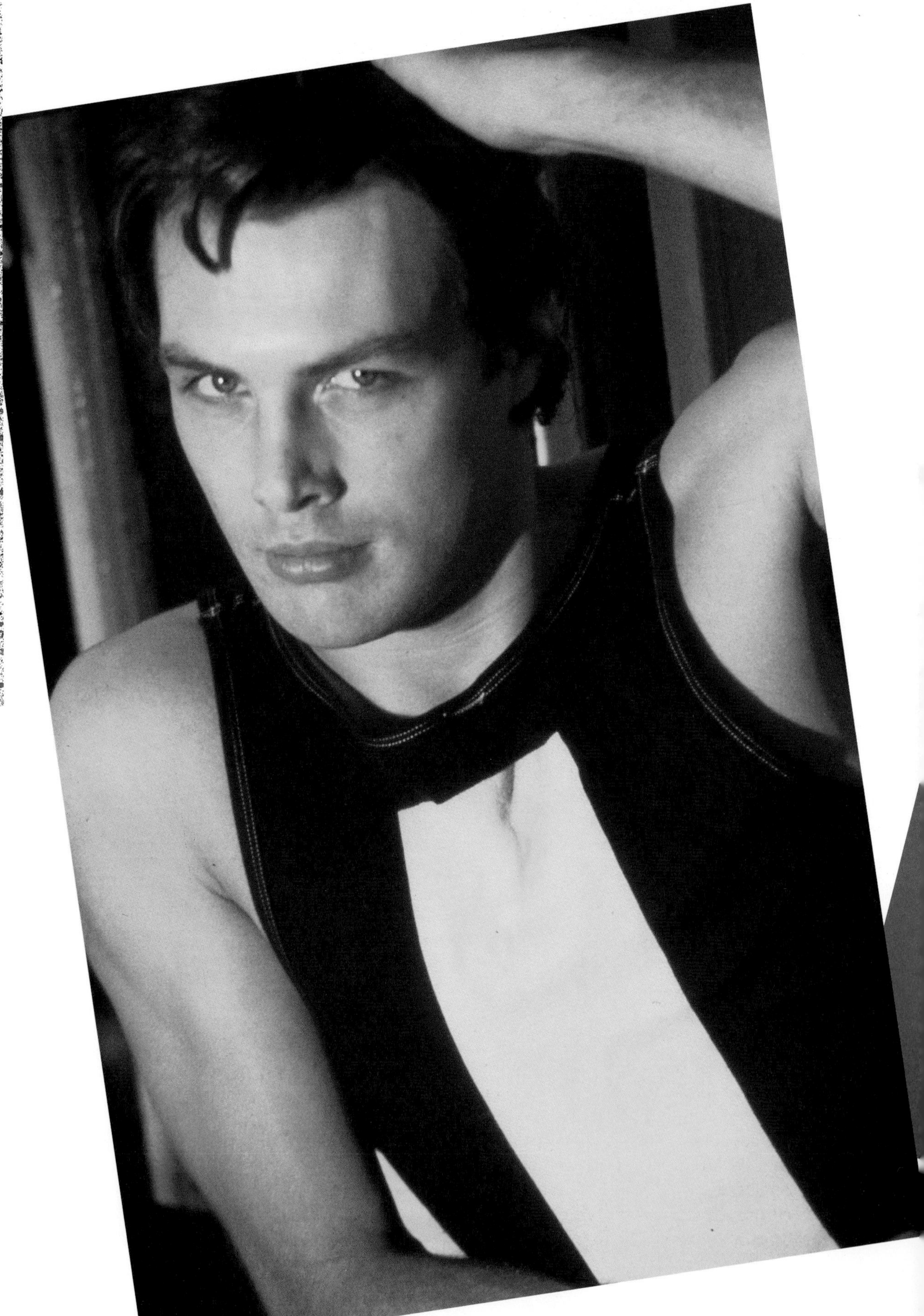

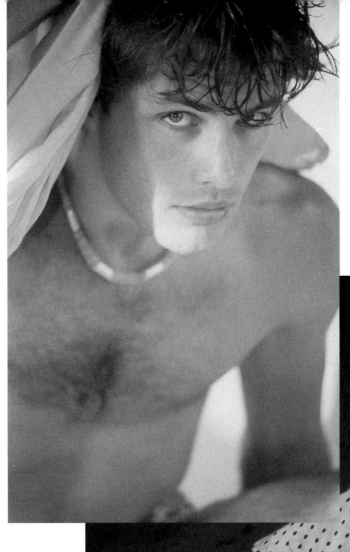

Ambitions: I'd like to make lots of money, but not just for the sake of making it, I'd like to plough my money into some environmentally useful project. My education broadened my mind sufficiently that I can go out and follow up things I'm interested in.

Fitness: My attitude to serious fitness training is '*mañana*', but I'm involved in martial arts and I do a lot of swimming.

My attitude to serious fitness training is 'mañana'.

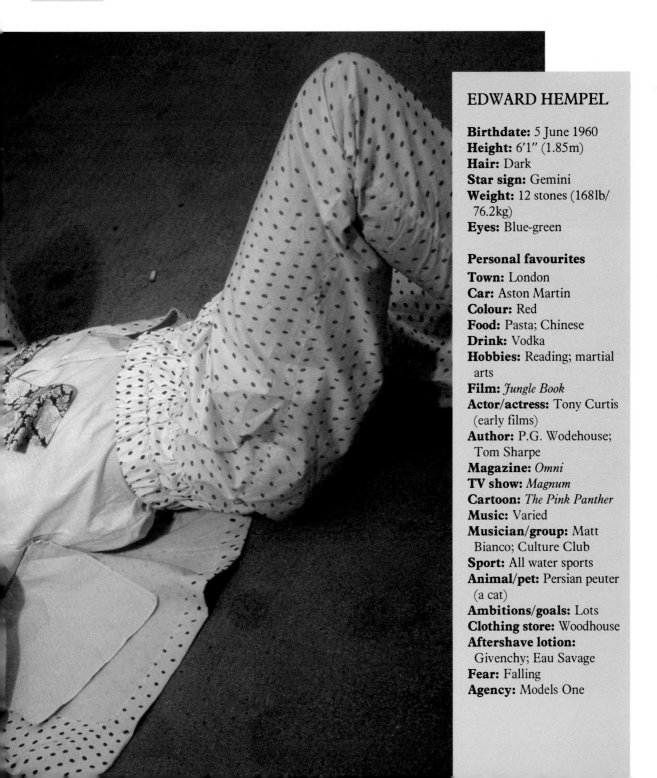

EDWARD HEMPEL

Birthdate: 5 June 1960
Height: 6′1″ (1.85m)
Hair: Dark
Star sign: Gemini
Weight: 12 stones (168lb/
 76.2kg)
Eyes: Blue-green

Personal favourites
Town: London
Car: Aston Martin
Colour: Red
Food: Pasta; Chinese
Drink: Vodka
Hobbies: Reading; martial
 arts
Film: *Jungle Book*
Actor/actress: Tony Curtis
 (early films)
Author: P.G. Wodehouse;
 Tom Sharpe
Magazine: *Omni*
TV show: *Magnum*
Cartoon: *The Pink Panther*
Music: Varied
Musician/group: Matt
 Bianco; Culture Club
Sport: All water sports
Animal/pet: Persian peuter
 (a cat)
Ambitions/goals: Lots
Clothing store: Woodhouse
Aftershave lotion:
 Givenchy; Eau Savage
Fear: Falling
Agency: Models One

CRISTOFER
AHRENS

Cristofer Ahrens now lives in London but was born in Atlanta, Georgia, of Norwegian and German parents.

Early ambitions: I wanted to be a professional tennis player. I travelled round the tennis tournaments in Europe and America, but it was just too tough and I wasn't good enough to make a living out of it. I won a lot of trophies, but international competition is cut-throat and there are thousands of people all trying to make a living out of it. So when the opportunity arose I switched careers.

Modelling: It seems models become popular just because they cross the ocean. American models are in demand in Britain and European models do very well in America once they've been to Milan and succeeded there.

London: I love London. It's my favourite city and I feel very at home here. It's like a large San Francisco, with so much culture – a lot of theatre, rock bands and films.

San Francisco's a nice town too but it's a bit small – there's not that much going on.

Working out: I work out in the gym five days a week on a regular programme to improve my body. The trouble is you can get too large and I've lost five jobs that I know of within three weeks because I can't get into standard-size shirts and suits. I think I'll concentrate on my legs for a bit now.

Ambitions: I want to be an actor eventually and plan to take some courses and move to Los Angeles. But, like modelling, acting is very competitive; it's who you know, having the right connections, being in the right place at the right time . . . and even then it's the luck of the draw.

It seems models become popular just because they cross the ocean.

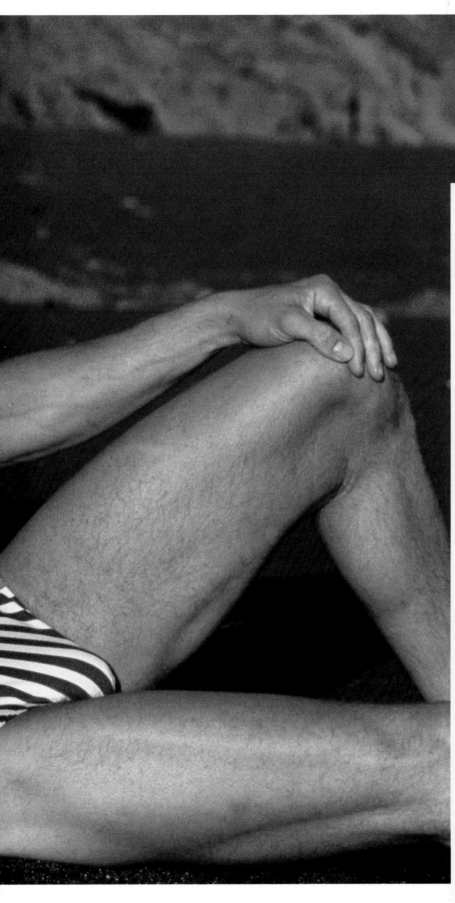

CRISTOFER AHRENS

Birthdate: 12 July 1956
Height: 6'2" (1.87m)
Hair: Blond
Star sign: Cancer
Weight: 12 stones (168lb/
  76.2kg)
Eyes: Hazel

Personal favourites
Time of day: Night
Town: London
Car: Jaguar XKE
Colour: Red
Food: Fish
Drink: Beer
Hobbies: Tennis
Film: *Sophie's Choice*; *Das
  Boot*
Actor/actress: Dustin
  Hoffman; Meryl Streep
Book: *Cancer Ward*
  (Solzhenitsyn)
Author: Dostoyevsky
Magazine: *Foreign Affairs*
Hero/heroine: Sam
  Sheppard
Music: New wave
Places to go: Theatre;
  good films
Holiday spots: Lake Tahoe
  in California
Sport: Tennis; body-
  building
Sportsman/woman: John
  McEnroe; Chris Lloyd
Ambitions/goals: To be
  an actor
Clothing designer:
  Marithe; Francois Girbaud
Fear: World war
Agency: Models One

G LEN
D AVIS

G *len Davis was born and brought up in*
Hastings, East Sussex.

Childhood: My dad threw me into the sea when I
was about 3 and I've swam ever since. My grandfather
was an Olympic swimmer so he was always swimming
miles out to sea with me at Hastings. When I was
about 9 a friend and I used to do high diving off the
end of the pier. We used to put on a show for all the
old ladies having tea, disappearing 50 feet over the
edge, then one of us would go round with a hat.

School: My school record isn't good. I could never
see the point of learning what happened to Henry VIII
and his six wives. They never teach you things at
school like human behaviour and how people react.
The first thing they should teach you is how to handle
people.

Dancing: I love dancing and have a job doing two
shows a night, six nights a week, in Soho. I don't take
drugs or drink because I just get high dancing. Some
of my dancing friends suggested I try modelling,
which is how I ended up as a model.

44

Modelling: I really enjoy modelling but I expect I'll move on to something else next. You reach frontiers, then you've got to find new ones, or life becomes boring. I'm good at making people laugh. I should have been a comedian.

I could never see the point of learning what happened to Henry VIII . . .

GLEN DAVIS

Birthdate: 14 April 1962
Height: 5'11½" (1.81m)
Hair: Brown
Star sign: Aries
Weight: 11½ stones (161lb/
  73.03kg)
Eyes: Brown

Personal favourites
Time of day: 2am
Town: Hastings
Car: 1937 Bugatti
Colour: Blue
Food: Chinese
Drink: Perrier water
Hobbies: Dancing; singing;
  swimming
Film: *Singing in the Rain*
Actor/actress: Sylvester
  Stallone
Book: *Here Today, Gone
  Tomorrow* (P. Broomsleigh)
TV show: *The 'A' Team*
Cartoon: Tom & Jerry
Places to go: Rio de
  Janeiro and Mexico
Sport: Swimming; weight-
  lifting
Sportsman/woman: Daley
  Thompson
Animal/pet: Tiger
Ambitions/goals: To be
  an actor
Aftershave lotion: Eau
  Sauvage
Fantasy: Being a pop star
Agency: Nev's

*K*EVIN
*A*RNDT

*B*orn and brought up in Bexley, Kent,
Kevin Arndt studied computers, electronics
and mathematics at City University,
London. After graduating he worked in the
City as a commodity trader in the sugar
trade, buying and selling for clients
worldwide.

School: I was always very academic but I
just decided I didn't want to push
formulas all my life – I wanted something
different.

Modelling: I was at a night club in
London and someone asked me if I wanted
to do a fashion show, which I did, and
ended up modelling. I've travelled all over
the place and I like modelling because it
gives you a lot of flexibility and a lot of
time to do things you want. It gives you
time to think, to plan your life a bit, rather
than have all the routine of a normal job.

I'm always eating – people seem to think I train a lot when they see me, but I don't.

48

Keeping fit: I don't consciously keep fit. I love to eat out and I'm always eating – I'm basically a pig! People seem to think I train a lot when they see me, but I don't. I have to watch I don't get too muscular for modelling, otherwise none of the standard sizes fit.

Sport: I've done a lot of sprinting and used to train with the squad at Crystal Palace when I was at university. I was actually training with a guy who came 5th in the Olympics, and I did train for some Internationals, but I felt I should either go for it properly or not at all, so I gave it up.

Ambitions: My ambition is to achieve things in whatever I do. After modelling I'd like to concentrate on becoming a good actor. At the same time I would put my money into a property business – I don't want to work for anyone else and I think the way to make money is to be a bit of an entrepreneur.

49

KEVIN ARNDT

Birthdate: 9 July 1961
Height: 6'1½'' (1.87m)
Hair: Dark brown
Star sign: Cancer
Weight: 12½ stones (175lb/
79.39kg)
Eyes: Blue

Personal favourites
Time of day: Evening
Town: Bray
Car: Convertible 'E'-type
Jaguar
Colour: Blue
Food: Fish
Drink: Whisky
Hobbies: Cars; athletics;
eating out
Film: *One Flew Over the
Cuckoo's Nest*
Actor/actress: Paul
Newman; Clint Eastwood;
Jack Nicholson
Book: *Catcher in the Rye*
(J.D. Salinger)
Author: J.D. Salinger
Magazine: *Gentleman's
Quarterly*
TV show: *Not the Nine
O'Clock News*
Hero/heroine: Muhammad
Ali
Cartoon: Tom & Jerry
Music: Soul; blues
Musician/group: Roy
Ayres; Ronnie Laws
Sport: Athletics
Sportsman/woman: Alan
Wells
Animal/pet: Cat
Ambitions/goals: To
achieve success as an actor
Clothing store: Gianni
Versace
Clothing designer: Gianni
Versace; Calvin Klein
Aftershave lotion: Paco
Rabanne
Fantasy: Being an Olympic
gold medallist
Fear: Old age
Agency: Nev's

D AVID *H* OSKIN

*B*orn and brought up in Adelaide, Southern Australia, David Hoskin came to England in 1974.

Home: Since I came to England when I was 16 I have only been back for four months. Adelaide was pretty conservative and quiet eleven-twelve years ago, but when I went back recently the place was so much more liberal. It just wasn't the place I expected – it was so down in the dumps when I left and it's really nice now.

Modelling: I was studying to be a surveyor in London when a friend suggested I should try modelling. That was in 1979 and things have certainly changed a lot in the business since then. I really wouldn't advise anyone to start modelling now because there are so many more people doing it and there is lots of competition. People in modelling now are more casual than in the past and of course there are younger guys doing it, which is the American influence. When I started

everyone was older than me at the agency. Modelling has its ups and downs but it has allowed me to see a lot of the world and work at the same time. I've been to America, the Caribbean and most of Europe. When I first started I went to Milan for three months which was fabulous – I love Italy. In fact I really like most of Europe, except for Greece and Spain.

Sports: I surf and swim when I can. If the client doesn't mind then I take my surfboard on trips. I surf in Cornwall as well. In the winter I love to ski. It was doing a ski commercial that really got me going. Now I organize a ski holiday every year for ten or twelve of us to go together.

Clothes: I have a standard wardrobe with a selection of shirts and trousers. You don't get given anything – clients always promise you things but you never get them. I like classic clothes best, not trendy clothes which are in one month and out the next.

Ambitions: I like the English people very much but would like to go back to Australia eventually and set up some sort of business. Australians are much more aggressive in their attitude towards work. In England they tend to sit back a lot more and wait for things to happen. I'll probably model until I'm 30. I've bought a house in London and I'm working well, so it would be silly to jeopardize anything just now.

A BAGGIER SPLASH

These floral-printed baggy cotton shorts with draw-string waists are derived from surfers' shorts of the early Sixties and are the dernier cri on beaches from Malibu to Mustique. All by Vilebrequin, about £20, from Joseph, 6 Sloane Street, SW1 and 16 South Molton Street, W1. Photographed by Nick Jarvis in Mustique.

DAVID HOSKIN

Birthdate: 14 May 1958
Height: 6′ (1.83m)
Hair: Fair
Star sign: Taurus
Weight: 12½ stones (175lb/
79.38kg)
Eyes: Blue

Personal favourites
Time of day: 5.30pm
Town: Brixton, London
Transport: Motorbike
Colour: Chrome
Food: Curry
Drink: Beer and Alka-
Seltzer (not together!)
Hobbies: Gambling
Film: *Texas Chainsaw
Massacre*
Actor/actress: Larry
Hagman
Book: *Field of Blood* (Gerald
Seymour)
Author: Jackie Collins
TV show: *Antiques Road
Show*
Hero/heroine: Ronald
Biggs
Cartoon: *The Flintstones*
Music: Loud heavy metal
Musician/group: Leonard
Cohen
Places to go: The Prince
Regent pub
Holiday spots: Isle of Man
Sport: Darts
Sportsman/woman:
Marvin Hagler
Animal/pet: Gerbil
Ambitions/goals: To go
free-fall parachuting
Clothing store: Milletts
Clothing designer: Ben
Sherman
Aftershave lotion: Brut
Fantasy: Driving at
160mph on my motorbike
Fear: Prohibition
Agency: Nev's

CLIVE WILLIAMS

Born in Brighton and brought up in Surrey, Clive Williams, who has three brothers, left school at 16. He studied electronics at college for three years, then got a job with the Ministry of Defence in weapons. After taking voluntary redundancy, he modelled for picture magazines and eventually joined a model agency. He combines modelling with working as a fitness instructor in Covent Garden. He is a Black Belt 1st Dan in karate.

School: I remember a couple of teachers whacking me round the ears at school because I couldn't get anything right. When I was 15 my teachers discovered I was dyslexic.

Modelling: I'm not the sort of person that ever wanted to be a model. I wouldn't recommend it as a career unless you've got the right attitude of mind. You can get very taken in with it all. If you haven't got a strong sense of values you can get led up the garden path. Some of the girls, for instance, are coming in at 16 having never had any other job and are on high earnings straight away; they haven't got any sense of the value of money so they just spend it furiously and at the end they're left with nothing.

Fitness: Becoming a fitness instructor was a natural progression for me. I've always been interested in fitness. I teach all ages, sexes, sizes. Recently I taught a girl with multiple sclerosis – she was one of the bravest people I've ever met. She could barely walk and was in great pain, yet she made herself do the exercises.

Cookery: I cook for myself, and I like cooking exotic dishes – steamed fish and stir-fried food. I eat a lot of fish but don't touch meat very often.

Sports: When I was at school I hated football and rugby. I couldn't see the point of all that grappling, pushing and shoving. My brother was a very good rugby player but he was always coming home with something broken. So I turned to karate.

Home: I've just bought a house in Chertsey, Surrey. It's a really pretty little village dating back to the fourteenth century, with its own museum. The house is Grade II listed with a big open fireplace and I knew before I even looked upstairs that it was what I wanted, so I made an offer on the spot.

I'm not the sort of person that ever wanted to be a model.

CLIVE WILLIAMS

Birthdate: 12 June 1958
Height: 6′ (1.83 m)
Hair: Fair
Star sign: Gemini
Weight: 12½ stones (175 lb/ 79.38 kg)
Eyes: Blue

Personal favourites
Time of day: Sunrise
Town: Sydney
Car: Aston Martin DB5
Colour: Electric blue
Food: Japanese
Drink: Apple juice
Hobbies: Martial arts; drumming; being a gym instructor; motorbikes; restoring furniture
Film: *Enter the Dragon*
Actor/actress: Clint Eastwood
TV show: *Hill Street Blues*
Cartoon: Tom & Jerry
Music: Anything rhythmical; not country & western or folk music
Places to go: Australia
Holiday spots: Anywhere secluded, with sun and sea
Sport: Boxing; motorcycling
Sportsman/woman: Geoff Capes; Brian Jackson; Daley Thompson
Animal/pet: Fish (has tropical fish at home)
Ambitions/goals: To be a successful actor
Fantasy: Owning a hot island with my own laws and rules
Fear: Being crippled
Agency: Nev's

R OEL

K UNST

From Friesland in the north of Holland ('where the best cows come from'), Roel Kunst is now based in London.

Starting out: I was playing in a band in Amsterdam a few years ago and I got an opportunity to play in England. We started playing in Bristol, which wasn't a great success. We were fighting the record companies, trying to get a break, and starving at the same time. I ended up in London and got the opportunity to become a model. I'm still at the stage where everything is interesting and a lot of new things are happening to me . . .

Modelling: It's a job that gets into you. It's good pay, pretty easy work and you meet so many people – which I really like. I can't really find a good alternative to it. On the other hand, I'm beginning to feel irritated after living out of a suitcase for the past couple of years.

When you start modelling you need at least a year-and-a-half to get established with clients. London is a

good city to begin in because clients are more relaxed than they are in Paris or Milan. Most of the models in France and Italy are Americans, which is probably the fault of the Parisian agencies. They take on so many Americans fresh from the beach who arrive in Paris, spend all their savings then call home to ask for more money. They don't want to go back until they've seen Europe, so they go to Milan, where everyone ends up, and you have to be really lucky to get work amongst that crowd. However, the Italian clients do have more imagination than their English counterparts. In Milan you can just walk into a room and they will know exactly what they want, even if you have no pictures with you. In Britain, clients want to see a prepared book and are only interested in pictures with writing on, ones that have been used in magazines.

The Japanese: Recently I was working in Japan, where you need a bit of time to acclimatize to a completely different culture and way of thinking, which shocked me at first because the Japanese never speak the truth . . . you never find a Japanese who is frank with you. They never speak about themselves, even to a friend, so it's very difficult to find out about them and what they are thinking, or what they are thinking about *you*. It's difficult with money, too, because there is so much corruption and black money floating around. And they drink like mad as well!

Family: My family is still in Holland. Funnily enough, the older you get the more contact you try to make with your family.

Languages: As we are such a small country all Dutch people have to speak many languages in order to survive. We all learn English, French and German to a high standard at school.

The Dutch *vs.* the British: Everyone in Holland is involved in politics and it's probably the most liberated country in Europe. I found when I came to London there is still an incredible difference between rich and poor and I see that people are actually starving in Britain. In Holland there is a minimum social security payment of £300 a month; for families it is more, so nobody starves there. However, I'm also more critical of Holland now that I'm living abroad. I trained as a teacher over there and when I stopped teaching I got £500 a month social benefit, which I just couldn't cope with. I see my friends there now just sitting around, wasting their lives and missing out on life. There is a lot of decadence amongst young Dutch people and I had to leave the country to see it clearly.

I have tried to find out why the English people think like they do and have studied a bit of English history. A class system would never work in Holland, but in Britain it does because of the old-fashioned laws and traditions and also the popularity of the monarchy. Young people in Holland have no respect for the royal family. We have a pretty good government system and we don't need a monarchy.

Clothes: I'm not interested in designer clothes at all. I like them and can see the beauty of them, but I just cannot spend so much money on clothes. So I usually wear secondhand jackets and I particularly like Marks & Spencer's pyjamas during the day.

ROEL KUNST

Birthdate: 28 August 1958
Height: 6'1" (1.85m)
Hair: Brown
Star sign: Virgo
Weight: 11¾ stones
  (164.5lb/74.61kg)
Eyes: Green/brown

Personal favourites
Time of day: Early
  morning
Town: Amsterdam
Food: Italian
Drink: Belgian beer
Hobbies: Music
Film: *La Strada* (Fellini)
Actor/actress: Jessica
  Lange
Book: *Noble House* (James
  Clavell)
Author: Gore Vidal
Hero/heroine: James
  Bond; Sophia Loren
Musician/group: Chaka
  Khan
Sport: Martial arts
Ambitions/goals: Not to
  get stressed
Clothing store: Pashu
Clothing designer: Gianni
  Versace
Aftershave lotion: Chanel
Fantasy: A lot
Fear: Bitchy clients
Agency: Laraine Ashton –
  IFM

M ALLORY
K AUDERER

B orn and brought up in Philadelphia, Mallory Kauderer was studying bio-chemistry at university when he was approached by a photographer to do some modelling.

Modelling: Over a two-month period I realized I was doing more modelling work than studying, so I had a break from my degree course. (I'll go back and finish it later, though – I just need about 25 credits to make up the total of 125 credits for a degree in the American system.) I then left

Modelling's a good job – you can make a lot of money, travel the world and have a good time.

Philadelphia and went to New York. After that I came to London, and since then I've been all over Europe and the rest of the world. I like to work in Europe better than the States, so London is a perfect place to live – it's a nice city, everyone speaks English and I like the lifestyle here. I wouldn't want to live in Paris, and certainly not Milan, which is a big, dirty city where all the bad things in this business are. Everyone needs Milan – credits there mean prestige – but if you do well there it doesn't necessarily mean you'll do well elsewhere. Milan uses a certain sort of model with a certain style and look, not so much commercial, which is what you have to be for the rest of the world.

Over-exposure: Work generates more work, but you can get to the point where you're over-saturated. If your face appears on posters all over the place and you become identified with one company, then other clients won't use you. I'm sure it's harder for models to get started now, though, because it's getting over-crowded. There are too many models for not enough jobs. If you can do well at it, then it's a good job – you can make a lot of money, travel the world and have a good time.

Work generates more work, but you can get to the point where you're over-saturated.

Girlfriends: In this business you meet so many girls . . . in the end I got tired of going out with just models. A lot of them aren't interested in anything outside modelling, and it's boring at the end of the day only talking about work. I've just bought an old house in Fulham and am going to settle down for a while with a girl who is a singer. Marriage is still a long way off for me — if I want to have kids then I'll get married, otherwise I see no reason to.

MALLORY KAUDERER

Birthdate: 16 September 1960
Height: 6′ (1.82m)
Hair: Brown
Star sign: Virgo
Weight: 12 stones (168lb/ 76.2kg)
Eyes: Blue

Personal favourites
Time of day: Suppertime
Town: Martha's Vineyard
Car: Mustang convertible
Colour: Blue
Food: Japanese
Drink: Beer
Hobbies: Reading; chess; eating
Film: *Dr Zhivago*
Actor/actress: Harrison Ford; Meryl Streep
Book: *Lord of the Rings* (Tolkien)
Author: Tolkien
Magazine: *Esquire*
TV show: *M.A.S.H.*
Cartoon: *Garfield*
Music: All
Musician/group: James Taylor
Holiday spots: Big, beautiful beaches
Sport: Basketball
Sportsman/woman: Chris Lloyd
Ambitions/goals: Wealth; contentment
Clothing designer: Stephen King
Fantasy: Flying on the space shuttle
Fear: To die young or to grow old
Agency: Nev's

JOSEPH YEO

Born in Kuala Lumpur, Malaysia, to a Chinese father and an Irish mother, Joseph Yeo is a qualified engineer and a dancer as well as a professional model.

Family background: My father was a lieutenant colonel in the Malaysian army and he came to England to study at Sandhurst. He had a holiday romance in Ireland and dragged my mother home to Malaysia, where they married. I was brought up there with my brother and sister. English was our natural language but we also spoke Malay at school. The country is made up of many nationalities and each night the same news is read in English, Malay, Chinese and an Indian language.

When I was 13 my parents split up and I returned to Ireland, to live in Dublin with my mother and sister. I went to secondary school in Dublin and ended up

with an engineering degree at Trinity College, Dublin.

Modelling: I then worked in tele-communications for two years as a project manager, but in my spare time I was doing a lot of mime and dancing – ballet, tap and modern. Eventually I gave up my job and came to London. I did some dancing at fashion shows and tried to get into the modelling business. I was refused by ten agencies! I then looked more carefully at how I should present myself – I changed my pictures, photographers, clothes, style, and adopted a more professional approach. Then I was accepted straight away.

To begin with I had to groom myself to look more European and on some pictures it's impossible to tell that I am Chinese. I'm going to model in Singapore soon, though, where my natural looks will be popular.

Food: One of my great passions is food. There is more variety in Malaysian food than in any other cuisine. Recently I spent two months there and never ate the same meal twice. The seafood, in particular, is wonderful – plenty of lobster, crab and king prawns, which somehow taste more succulent and fresh than when I have eaten them in Europe.

I was refused by ten agencies!

Showbusiness: In my spare time I'm working on a special act which incorporates all my resources as an engineer, model and dancer. It is a very sophisticated robotic act based on movement, colour and sound. In most robotic acts people just wear boiler suits and paint their faces white, but I want people to think this is not just a guy looking like a robot, it's a robot imitating a man. I wear a shiny black suit full of metal bars and wires and cables and I have a computer inside which controls all the lights and the metal laser gun. There is a specially recorded original soundtrack and at the end I pull off my mask and reveal a face full of wires – it's very effective.

JOSEPH YEO

Birthdate: 29 October 1960
Height: 6′ (1.83 m)
Hair: Dark brown/black
Star sign: Scorpio
Weight: 11½ stones (161 lb/ 73.03 kg)
Eyes: Brown

Personal favourites

Time of day: 3 am
Town: Paris
Car: Lamborghini
Colour: Black
Food: Chow quey deon (Malaysian/Chinese dish)
Drink: Pils lager
Hobbies: Special effects; eating out; beach bumming
Actor/actress: Harrison Ford; Jessica Lange
Magazine: *Omni*
Hero/heroine: Errol Flynn
Music: Funk; rock
Places to go: Restaurants; nightclubs
Holiday spots: Monaco; Malaysia
Sport: Swimming
Ambitions/goals: As I am a Scorpio my ambitions remain a secret
Clothing store: Brown's
Clothing designer: Montana; Pancietti
Aftershave lotion: Gianni Versace
Fantasy: This week, it's Raquel Welch in a rubber dress
Fear: Heights and boredom
Agency: Gavin's

CHARLES WINSLOW

Charles Winslow was born in Chicago, brought up in the Mid-West and went to school on the east coast. Though his parents now live in Japan, he keeps an eye on his three younger brothers when he is in New York.

Career path: I had just got a job working in computer systems with an accounting firm in New York, which I was due to start in the autumn. That summer I went to New Orleans in Louisiana and worked in a bar. I was approached there to be a model but I said I wasn't interested. I had my life all planned. So the guy said, 'Why not just try and make some extra money while you're bartending?' So I did, and in my first job I made a huge sum in one week, more than I would have been paid in three months in my new computer job. So I thought, right, I'll do this now and go back to computers later.

Modelling: I've been modelling for two-and-a-half years now but I'd like to go to business school in New York next year and perhaps continue to model at the same time. I enjoy the travel and the freedom of modelling but I don't enjoy the actual process. Sometimes it's good, but the majority of modelling is

studio work or catalogue work, not with the greatest photographer or greatest clothing or greatest location. The income is what keeps you in it – most other jobs just don't pay like that.

Work locations: Before I came to England I had three or four months in Milan which I liked very much as I also speak Italian. I've worked in different parts of England so I've had a chance to see Oxford, Bath and the south coast, also many museums, and eat in lots of different restaurants.

Nationalities: The English are more civil than the Americans, though not as much fun in a mindless sort of way. Living in New York you can become obsessed with fun – parties every single night that end at 4 in the morning. You get up and go to work and then start all over again. It's a senseless pursuit of fun that's tiring rather than relaxing. The English have a slower, nicer lifestyle.

Humour: English humour is really quite interesting for Americans. Although Americans have a lot of fun and smile a lot, our humour is not as well developed as yours. Ours is more slapstick, whereas yours is based on puns, and plays on words and situations.

MALE
Magazine for the Innovative Man. *dansen* Extra Issue

特集 "男友達"

男たちは都会の海を泳いでいる

Photographer by Robert Mapthorpe

CHARLES WINSLOW

Birthdate: 15 March 1960
Height: 6′ (1.89m)
Hair: Brown
Star sign: Pisces
Weight: 11½ stones
 (164.5lb/75.61kg)
Eyes: Blue

Personal favourites
Time of day: 11pm
Car: Jaguar XKE
 Convertible
Colour: British racing
 green
Food: Japanese; shellfish
Drink: Beer
Hobbies: Racket sports;
 skiing
Film: *Back to the Future*
Author: James Mitchener
Magazine: *The Economist*
TV show: *The Two Ronnies*
Hero/heroine: Richard
 Stockman
Cartoon: *Bugs Bunny*
Music: Classical
Musician/group: Old Bob
 Dylan
Places to go: La Costa
 Esmeralda
Sport: Tennis; skiing;
 water-skiing
Clothing designer:
 Armani
Fear: Being 30 and still a
 model
Agency: Models One

I AN *C* OCHRANE

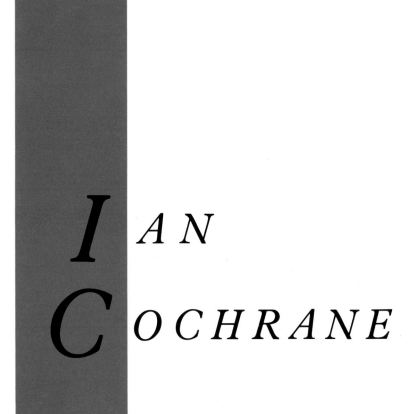

A Scot from Airdrie, Ian Cochrane is the youngest of five children. He has a sister in Texas and three brothers in New York, Oman and London. He joined the Navy straight from school and later managed a couple of betting shops in London. A former winner of the title 'Man of the UK', he has modelled all over the world, including America and South Africa. He keeps in shape by training most days. He appeared in the film Bolero *with Bo Derek but does not want to become an actor.*

Accent: When I first came to London people couldn't understand what I was saying. When I go home now people call me a foreigner.

Home: I was going to sign on with the Navy for nine years. After the first six months my sister came over from America and begged me not to join up, so I signed myself out and went back to America with her for six months. I enjoyed America for a holiday, but London is home now (though if there's a football match I still support Scotland).

Betting: I'm a bit of a gambler and for me it often used to mean no wages at the end of the week! Some you win, some you lose.

A model is just an everyday guy.

Fishing: Off Cape Town, I did some cray fishing, diving down under the rocks with no oxygen. What you do is put gloves on and grab them. It's a bit scary because you're trying to grab them before they grab you and the water makes them look bigger than they are. You can get killed doing this, because the crayfish wedge themselves under the rocks and hold you under.

Keeping fit: I don't like going to gyms. I'm a very private person, so I train in my own flat in Little Venice – I've got a lot of space and do asymmetrics and that kind of thing.

Modelling: I've always been a bit of a keep-fit fanatic and some friends said 'Why don't you go in for it?' I did, and I won. I had a lot of pictures taken and this started me in modelling. Modelling is not as glamorous as most people think. A model is just an everyday guy.

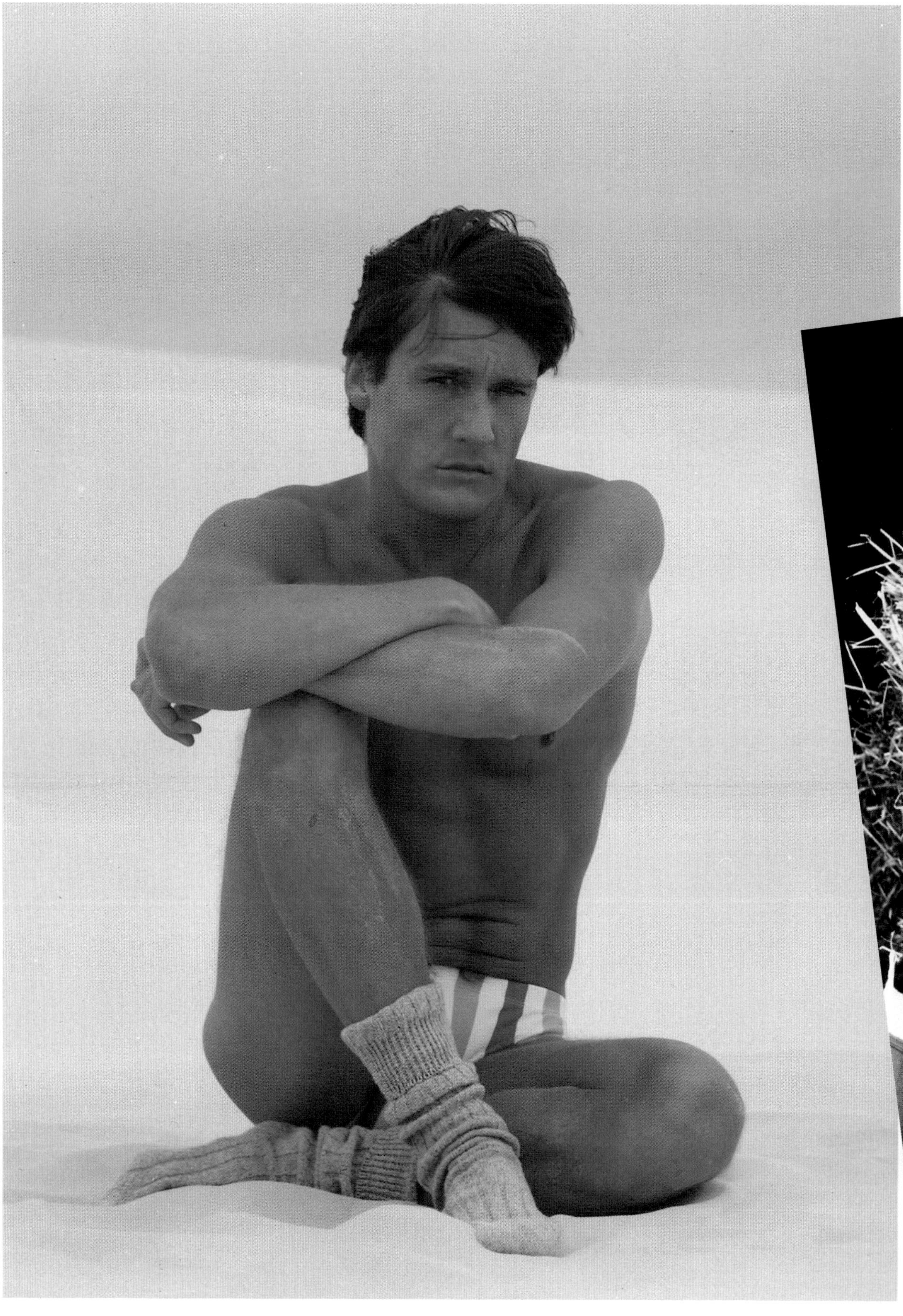

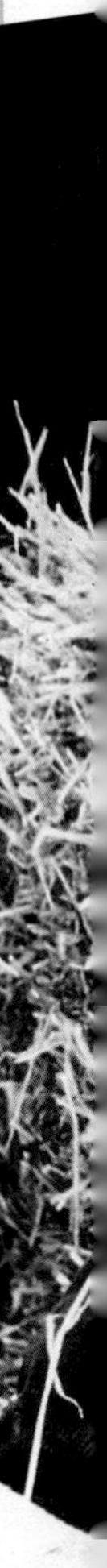

Gambling often used to mean no wages at the end of the week!

IAN COCHRANE

Birthdate: 9 September 1957
Height: 6' (1.89m)
Hair: Brown
Star sign: Virgo
Weight: 12 stones (168lb/76.2kg)
Eyes: Green-blue

Personal favourites
Time of day: Night
Town: London
Car: BMW
Colour: Red
Food: Very rare steak
Drink: Vodka
Hobbies: Training and sport; drinking
Actor/actress: James Garner
Book: *Taipan* (James Clavell)
Author: James Clavell
Magazine: *Vogue*
TV show: *The Rockford Files*
Hero/heroine: Superman
Musician/group: Phil Collins
Holiday spots: Greece
Sport: Badminton
Sportsman/woman: Daley Thompson
Animal/pet: Dog
Aftershave lotion: Quorum
Fantasy: Owning the Derby winner
Fear: Snakes
Agency: Models One

STEVE GRANT

Australian-born Steve Grant began modelling in 1981 and has worked in Italy, Crete, Spain, Portugal, Tenerife, on the French Riviera and in Britain, as well as in Australia. Other assignments have taken him to the Seychelles, for a swimwear shoot with Patrick Lichfield, on the QE2 for a tobacco company, to Kenya for a French aftershave advertisement and on the Orient Express for a whisky commercial. He is married to an English girl called Belinda.

Getting started: Someone I have always wanted to thank, because she is the person who got me started on my career, is Sylvia Rayner from *Cosmo* magazine. It was Sylvia I first wrote to in an attempt to find out how to approach an agency. If she were here now I'd give her a big kiss . . .

Childhood: Pre-pubescent life was filled with memorable (and, I'm sure, forgettable) circumstance; at times I wondered what life was all about, but one thing I have maintained and can't stress enough is that friendship is a commodity that should be cherished and valued forever.

Food: I love it! My two adorable flatmates in Sydney, Ava and Fiona, see to it that my tastebuds are always kept guessing. Actually Ava is the Torvill and Dean of cooking, and Fiona the Walter Mondale. Fiona keeps me supplied with jellybeans and Smarties, which I love.

Home: Most of the year I'm in London and working from there, every summer I come back to Australia. I live with Belinda in a large, comfortable apartment in Kensington, London, looking out over an acre of trees and plants which is our courtyard. In Sydney my home is a penthouse in Neutral Bay, overlooking Middle Harbour and our very beautiful Sydney Harbour.

Holidays: Our last holiday was on Hydra, one of the beautiful Greek islands. We have friends who own a bar there and it's wonderful to sit and drink kahlua, play backgammon and look out at the harbour. For good skiing, it's just got to be Alpbach, Austria – one of the prettiest places on earth.

STEVE GRANT

Birthdate: 27 March 1958
Height: 6'2" (1.88m)
Hair: Dark brown
Star sign: Aries
Weight: 'Just right'
Eyes: Blue

Personal favourites
Time of day: Late afternoon in spring
Town: Emsworth (West Hants)
Car: Torana A9X
Colour: Scarlet O'Hara's lips
Food: Vegetables and cherries
Drink: Kahlua with milk
Hobbies: Collecting cricket bats; long bike rides
Film: *A Night at the Opera*
Actor/actress: Dustin Hoffman; Katharine Hepburn
Book: *No Drums, No Trumpets* (Barry Wynne); *Gray's Anatomy*
Author: Robert Louis Stevenson; David Niven
Magazine: *GQ*; *Vogue*
Hero/heroine: Three Musketeers; Annie Oakley
Cartoon: *Bugs Bunny*
Musician/group: Beatles; Deep Purple; Barbra Streisand
Places to go: Lords cricket ground; the sauna
Holiday spots: Positano (Italy); French riviera
Sport: Scuba diving; cricket; darts
Sportsman/woman: Doug Walters; Chris Lloyd
Ambitions/goals: To stay a male; play for Chelsea at Wembley
Clothing store: Mason's (Sydney); Paul Smith (London)
Clothing designer: Gianni Versace
Fantasy: Driving my A9X at Bathurst
Fear: AIDS; first grey hair
Agency: Nev's

A NDREW
C OTE

*B*orn and bred in Alberta, Canada, Andrew Cote is now based in London.

Home: I come from a big, booming town in Alberta, a bit like Dallas. Alberta is very dry and invigorating. In the winter it's cold and crisp but it's always sunny – it might be minus 20 degrees but people are still outside skating and cross-country skiing. In the summer it's very hot and dry.

Education: I studied political science at university, which might eventually give me an opening into law or the media. I took a year off in the middle of university and went to Fiji, Tahiti, Hawaii, New Zealand, Australia, Singapore, Bangkok, Hong Kong and Tokyo. It was fantastic – I'd tell anyone to do it. I started modelling to begin with to help pay for university, then when I finished my degree I thought it would be a good way to see Europe and travel around. I'm taking it seriously now and giving it one hundred per cent, but at

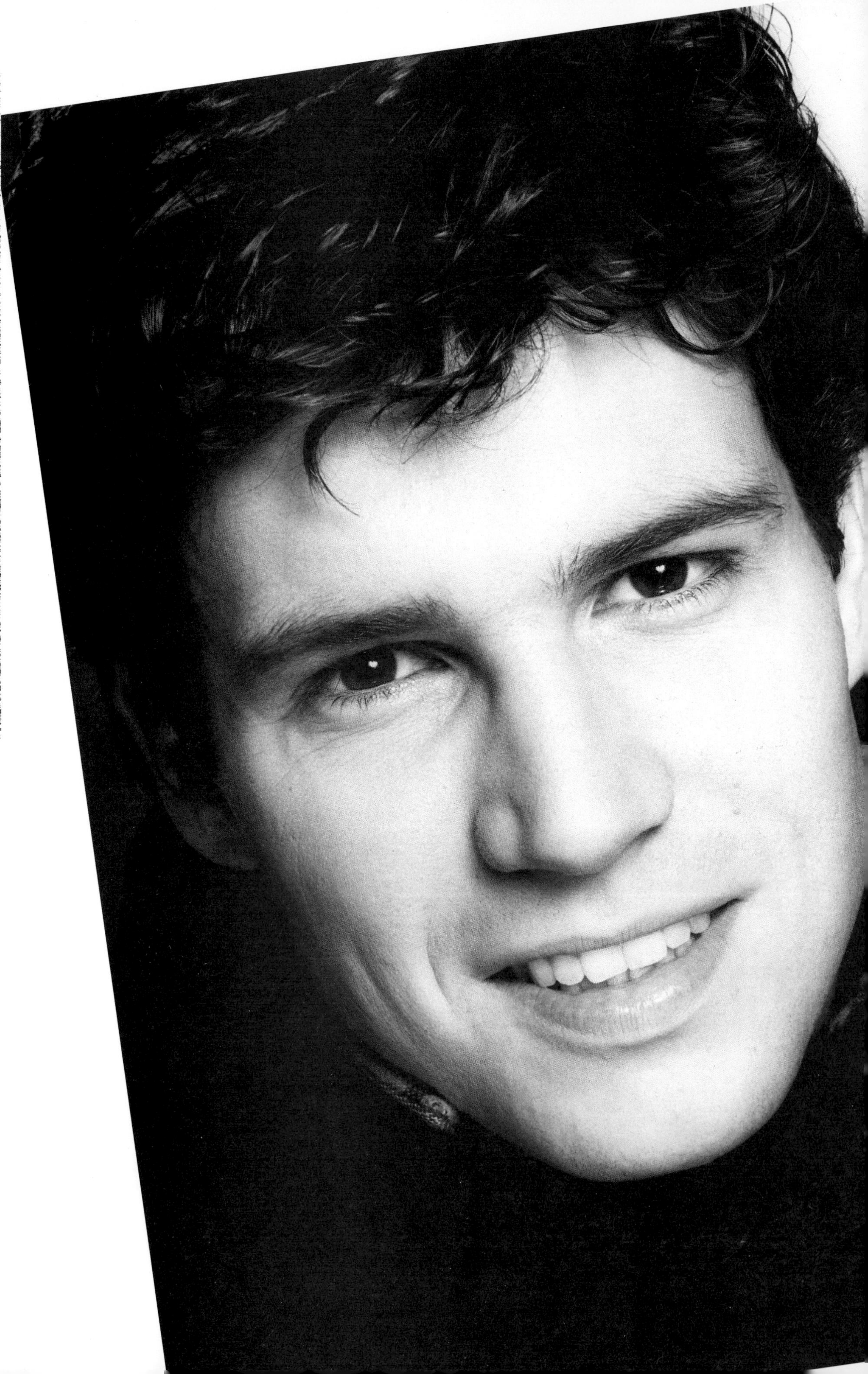

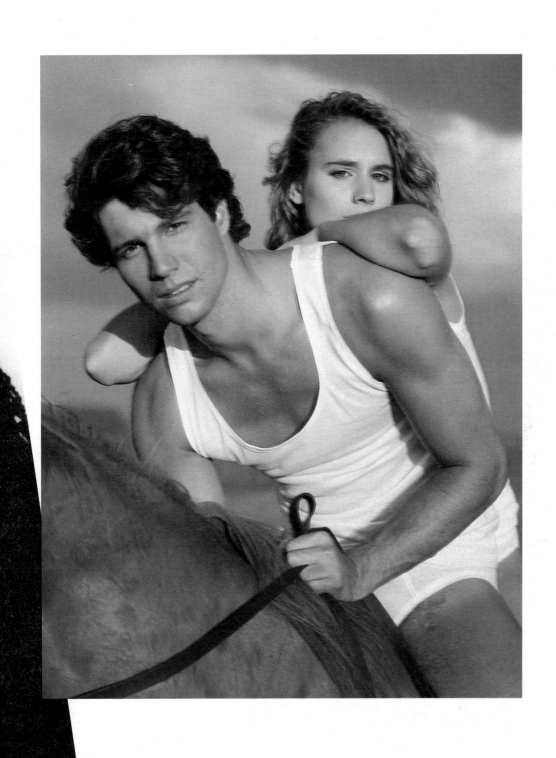

least if it doesn't work out I can always say it was a good experience and I saw so many different places in the world.

Fame: In Alberta I was in the paper a lot. In a small town you get to be pretty famous and everybody knows you, but in London you start right at the bottom. I love London. I could stay here too long, that's the problem.

Career aims: The ultimate place you want to work of course is New York, but you can't just go straight there. You have to do London, Paris, Hamburg, Milan, before they'll employ you in New York. I like doing commercial modelling best, in front of television cameras.

Fellow models: Other models I get on very well with. There are a lot of false suspicions about male models, but most of them are very nice guys. Although it's a very competitive field, nearly everyone is ready to give help and advice – for example, who to see and who not to see. It's not at all bitchy. Fashions of course are changing and it's not just the typically good-looking guy that always gets the work – there's a huge spectrum of what is considered fashionable and good-looking.

Clothes: I personally like wearing comfortable, baggy clothes best.

Fitness: I don't diet but I do a lot of exercise. When I can I ski, water-ski and play water-polo, but at the moment I'm into racket sports and the first thing I did when I reached London was join a sports club.

When I finished my degree I thought modelling would be a good way to see Europe and travel around.

It's not just the typically good-looking guy that always gets the work.

ANDREW COTE

Birthdate: 12 December 1961
Height: 6'2" (1.88m)
Hair: Brown
Star sign: Sagittarius
Weight: 12½ stones (175lb/ 79.38kg)
Eyes: Brown

Personal favourites
Time of day: Dawn or dusk
Town: Banff, Alberta
Car: Lotus Turbo Esprit
Colour: Candy apple red
Food: Seafood
Drink: Fresh mango
Hobbies: Sports; art; music
Film: *Amadeus*
Actor/actress: George C. Scott; Meryl Streep; Clint Eastwood
Book: *Pet Semetary* (Stephen King)
Author: Stephen King
Magazine: *Time*; *Newsweek*
TV show: *Dynasty*
Hero/heroine: Tarzan and Jane; my bookers
Cartoon: *Bugs Bunny*
Music: All, especially jazz
Musician/group: Al Jarreau
Places to go: South East Asia; Burma; Thailand
Holiday spots: Malibu; Monte Carlo; Southern France
Sport: Downhill; water-skiing
Sportsman/woman: John McEnroe
Animal/pet: Cats; lions
Ambitions/goals: To be rich and famous (or just rich)
Clothing store: Austin Reed
Clothing designer: Willi Smith/casual
Aftershave lotion: Royal Copenhagen/Drakkar Noir
Fantasy: Fast cars and beautiful women
Fear: Poverty; Mr T.
Agency: Models One

*B*OB *M*CQUILLEN

*B*orn and bred a Londoner, Bob McQuillen went to school down the Old Kent Road. He runs, swims and trains with weights every day.

Early ambitions: I originally wanted to be a fireman but during my last year at school I broke my arm badly a few times and damaged my knee, which stopped me getting into the Fire Service.

Working out: I've got into a system now: if I don't do it, I feel I'm missing out – it's like I've forgotten to clean my teeth.

Food: I don't diet, but I don't eat junk food.

Motorbikes: My big dream is to race them. In the summer I used to do dispatch riding. I had the biggest bike you can get, so I was always sent out on the longest jobs. I could make £300 to £400 a week riding round the countryside, stopping off at little pubs.

Modelling: I really enjoy modelling. I don't class it as a job. I'd do it for no money.

*I don't class
modelling as a job.
I'd do it for no
money.*

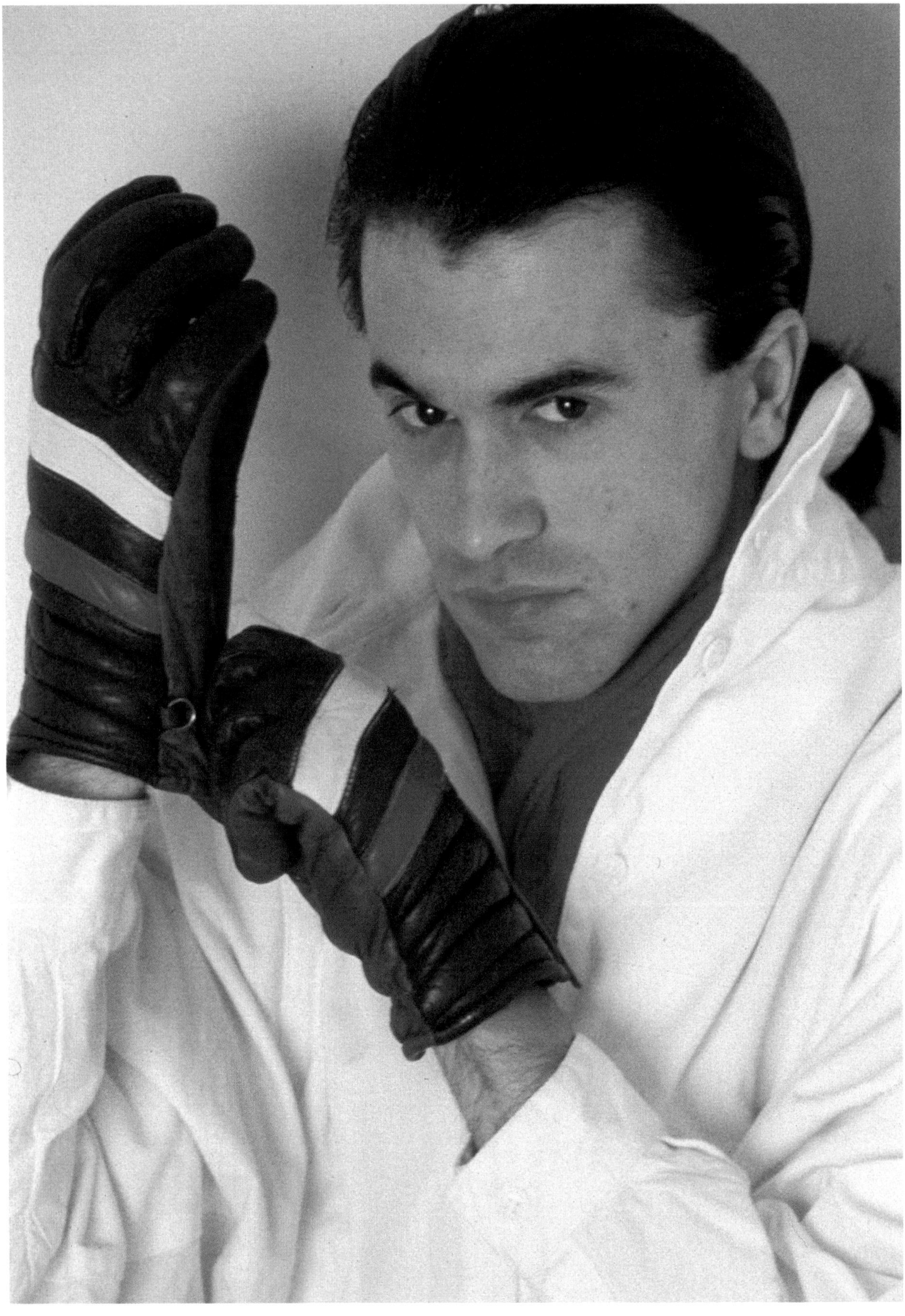

BOB McQUILLEN

Birthdate: 5 January 1961
Height: 6′1½″ (1.87m)
Hair: Brown
Star sign: Capricorn
Weight: 12 stones 2lb
 (170lb/77.11kg)
Eyes: Brown

Personal favourites
Time of day: Bedtime
Town: London
Car: Aston Martin
Colour: Black
Food: Steaks
Drink: Milk
Hobbies: Bikes; riding
 motorbikes
Film: *The Deer Hunter*
Actor/actress: John Hurt
Book: *Rich Man, Poor Man*
 (Irwin Shaw)
Author: James Herbert
Magazine: *Which Bike*
TV show: *The Young Ones*
Hero/heroine: Barry
 Sheene
Cartoon: Tom & Jerry
Music: Soul; jazz; rock;
 punk
Musician/group: Earth,
 Wind and Fire
Places to go: Clubs and
 wine bars; Brands Hatch
Sport: Boxing
Sportsman/woman: Barry
 Sheene
Animal/pet: Dog
Ambitions/goals: Fame
Clothing store: Brown's
Clothing designer:
 Johnson's
Fantasy: To make love to
 a woman from every
 country in the world
Fear: Breaking my neck
Agency: Gavin's Models

*If I don't work out it's
like I've forgotten to clean
my teeth.*

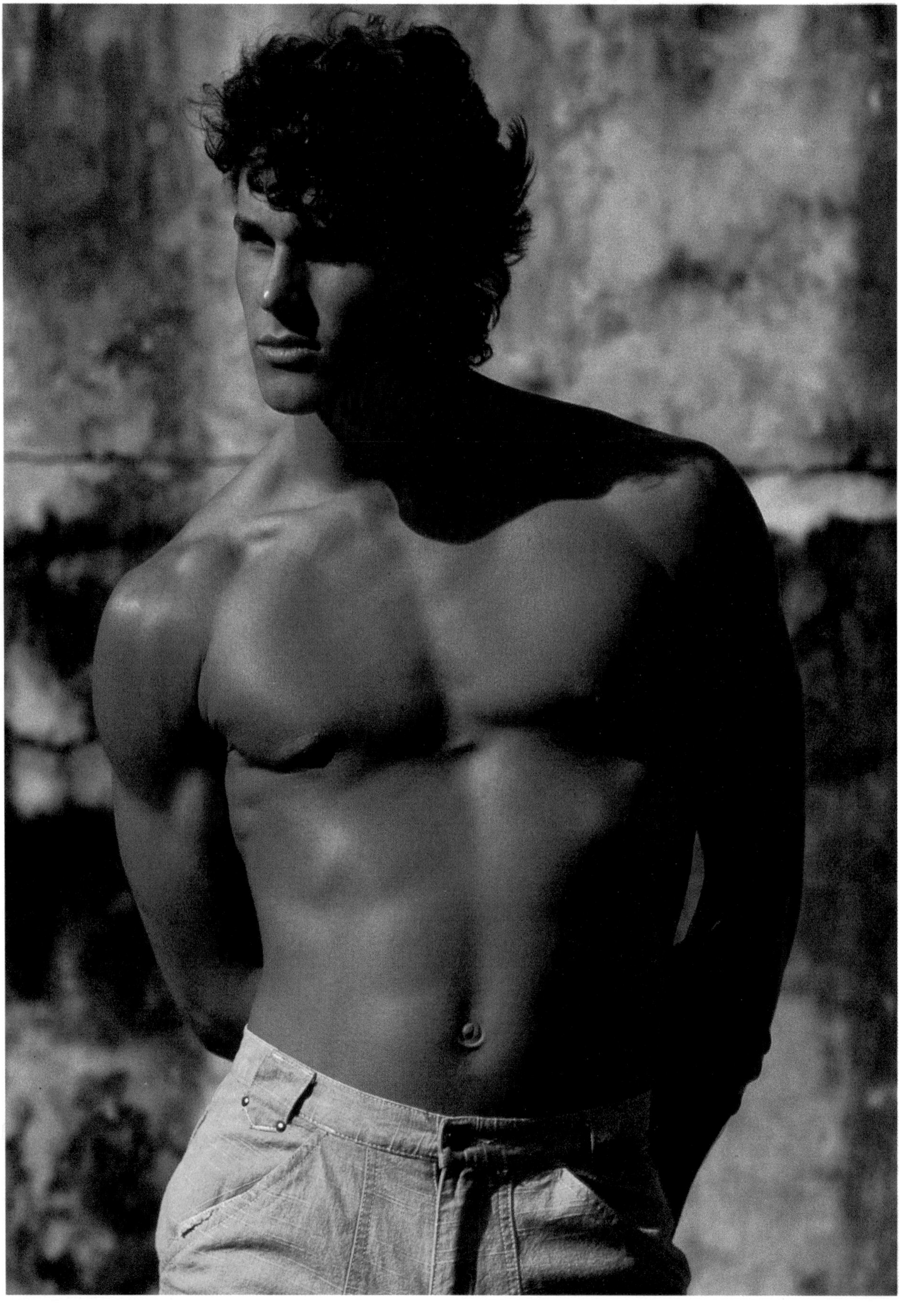

DAVID DONALD

David Donald went straight into modelling after A-levels at school.

Modelling: My first thoughts about it were when I was 17. I was going to university but I lost interest at school and didn't get the grades. I've worked a lot since I started modelling and went to the Bahamas and the Canaries in the first six months. I like doing TV commercials best – they're the most lucrative and you're on location.

Sports: I started water-skiing with the scouts when I was ten. We used to go on trips to Lake Windermere. I now water-ski every week at a club near Reading and take part in competitions. This year I'm hoping to buy my own proper competition ski boat with a friend, and with a better boat I'll be able to do some bigger regional competitions.

Hobby: I spend a lot of time working on my 3-litre Capri and I'm saving to build a replica AC Cobra.

Fitness: I used to play lots of football, rugby and athletics. Now I do about 100 press-ups a day to keep my physique as I like it.

Food: I eat anything and everything.

Ambitions: I like to think I could model for ten years or so. Eventually I want to start my own business if I've made enough money.

DAVID DONALD

Birthdate: 27 October 1965
Height: 6'1½" (1.87m)
Hair: Brown
Star sign: Scorpio
Weight: 13 stones (182lb/ 82.55kg)
Eyes: Brown

Personal favourites
Time of day: Evening
Town: Windsor
Car: AC Cobra 427
Colour: Black
Food: Pasta; anything and everything
Drink: Coca-cola
Hobbies: Water-skiing; all sports; cars
Film: *Midnight Express*
Actor/actress: Eddie Murphy
Magazine: *Car*
TV show: *Dallas* and good documentaries
Hero/heroine: Barry Sheene
Cartoon: Tom & Jerry
Music: Funk; soul
Musician/group: Maze; Luther Vandross; Wham!
Places to go: Busy pubs; parks
Holiday spots: Hawaii; Caribbean; Scottish highlands
Sport: Water-skiing
Sportsman/woman: Barry Sheene; Karl Lewis
Animal/pet: Dog (doberman)
Ambitions/goals: To control my own business
Clothing style: Casual and loose, but smart
Aftershave lotion: Paco Rabanne
Fantasy: Having lots of money
Fear: Poverty
Agency: Gavin's Models

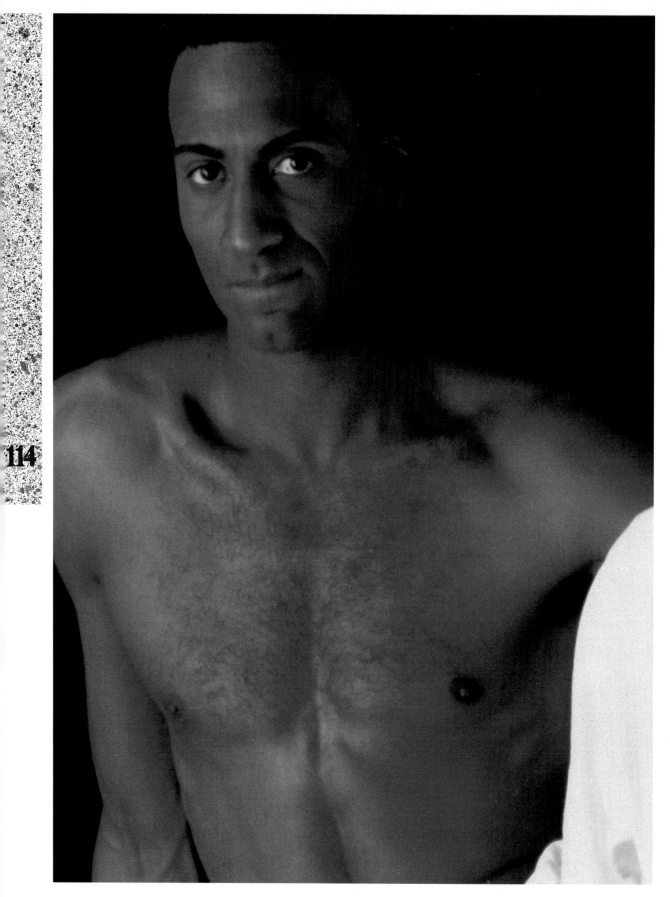

D AVID
C LAY

David Clay was born in Stepney, London, to a black father, whom he never saw, and a white mother who died of TB when he was small. He was brought up an orphan in a Catholic school on the Isle of Wight. He left the Catholic school at the age of 10, then, after convalescing from TB, went to live with guardians in the Kent countryside. He was the fastest runner in his Kent school, running for England as a junior against Holland. He now runs between modelling assignments for the Surrey Beagles and the Croydon Harriers in England, and for RRC in Holland (the 400-metre flat, 400-metre hurdles, 800 metres and relays), and has won the Kent County Championships at Crystal Palace. He was working as a vet's assistant when he was asked to join a black model agency. He now has homes in both Holland and England (London).

School: Catholic schools are the worst things possible. I got hit by the nuns when I did things wrong, and there were ridiculous rules like never being allowed to speak at mealtimes. If we spoke we had to stand and wait until everybody else had finished eating and then we could sit down and eat. Then there was a period of meditation when we had to sit on our beds for an hour-and-a-half, and when you're 9 or 10 that's very difficult. I do still

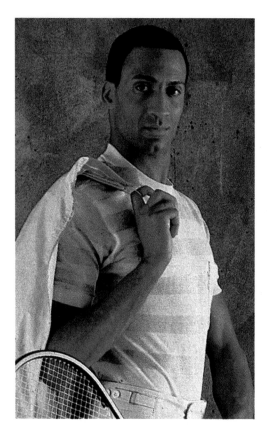

occasionally go to church and I do believe, but I have doubts about certain things.

Sport: I was the only black child in my village so I really had to prove myself. If you're a prefect or head boy people respect you more, but I was accepted through running. I don't run to keep fit, I run to win. I don't want to be second or third.

Modelling: I'd always thought of models as being a bit camp, so I was apprehensive to start with. Then one day I got a chance to do a big show in Berlin with models from all over Europe. I didn't know how to walk so I danced and got a lot of applause. I made more money on one show than in five weeks as a vet's assistant. After that I got more and more work and had to make a choice between modelling and going back to my vet's studies. I chose modelling and it's worked very well. I've worked in America, Russia and most European countries, and in England I've done shows for Harrods, Harvey Nichols, C & A and so on. I also do a lot of shows for charity. I've just done one for the Red Cross which made £51,000 for Ethiopia.

Being a black model can be difficult but it does also work for me. For instance, they often book a black male model with a couple of black female models for a show.

Business interests: I'm in partnership in a coffee shop in Amsterdam. All the magazine people come in, and the students, and also the tourists because it's just behind the Rijksmuseum.

Nationalities: I like Holland because it's central for getting to the rest of the Continent, and I like the Dutch because their mentality is almost the same as that of the English. The Germans are very starchy, the French are arrogant and the Italians are very highly strung to work with. The Dutch are laidback and crazy and I like that. I trained the Dutch chief of the Riot Police how to breathe and relax and jog for his modern pentathlon. His wife is a model and he came on trips to Spain with us when we made a commercial together, and we became good friends.

Ambitions: I would still like to go back to my vet's studies because my main ambition is to work in the country. I like London but it sometimes depresses me and I love to get out into the country where everything is so still and peaceful, because this is also where I was brought up – London and the country. When I die I'd like to say I've done everything. At 70 I don't want to say I wish I'd done more when I was young.

DAVID CLAY

Birthdate: 10 July 1952
Height: 6′3″ (1.90m)
Hair: Black
Star sign: Cancer
Weight: 11 stones (154lb/ 69.85kg)
Eyes: Brown

Personal favourites
Time of day: Any time
Town: Amsterdam
Car: Rolls-Royce
Colour: Blue; mauve
Food: Fish and cheesecake (not necessarily together)
Drink: Bad drinker: a little wine; milk
Hobbies: Athletics (have run for England); escaping to somewhere quiet
Actor/actress: Peggy Ashcroft; Meryl Streep
Book: *Lord of the Rings* (Tolkien)
Author: George Orwell
Magazine: *The Face*; *Athletics Weekly*
TV show: Any documentary
Hero/heroine: Duchess of Gloucester
Cartoon: *Popeye*
Music: Synthesized
Musician/group: Jean-Michel Jarre; Eurythmics
Places to go: Hever Castle in Kent (I love stillness)
Holiday spots: Nairobi – given the chance
Sport: Athletics
Ambitions/goals: To die smiling (but not yet)
Clothing store: Harrods
Clothing style: Second-hand clothes
Aftershave lotion: Anything that smells OK
Fear: Death
Agency: Gavin's Models

*M*ARK
*B*EISIEGEL

*B*orn and brought up in north London, Mark Beisiegel studied politics at Essex University before becoming a model.

Modelling: After I got a degree I left university not knowing what to do. I fancied something in the media but couldn't find a way in. I did some labouring jobs but I never expected to end up modelling. A friend who cuts my hair always has the different styles photographed, and the photographer advised me to try modelling. I had long hair then and none of the agencies was interested, but

You have to sell yourself in this world.

121

as soon as I had it cut very short I got accepted. Now, most of my friends take the mickey out of me! This kind of life is a completely different world to university, where we all had lot of idealistic notions, but unfortunately you have to sell yourself in this world.

Sports: I swim and play a lot of tennis and football and go to the gym four times a week. I cycled down to the south of France last summer, which should have been good fun except it rained non-stop – and it's not fun cycling in the rain.

Clothes: I like sports clothes best. I don't mind suits now and again, but it would drive me bananas to wear a suit in an office each day.

MARK C. BEISIEGEL

Birthdate: 2 August 1961
Height: 5'11" (1.8m)
Hair: Light brown
Star sign: Leo
Weight: 12¼ stones (172lb/ 78kg)
Eyes: Blue

Personal favourites
Time of day: Morning
Car: Austin A30
Colour: Green
Food: Granary bread
Drink: Orange juice
Hobbies: Reading; all sports
Film: *In the Heat of the Night*
Actor/actress: Walter Matthau; Meryl Streep
Book: *The Sea, the Sea* (Iris Murdoch)
Author: Iris Murdoch
Magazine: *The Face*
TV show: *Panorama*
Hero/heroine: Walter Matthau; Elizabeth Frink
Cartoon: Tom & Jerry
Music: Black music
Musician/group: Marc Almond
Places to go: Royal Academy of Arts, London
Holiday spots: St Jean de Luz, South of France
Sport: Tennis; football; cycling
Sportsman/woman: Sebastian Coe; Bjorn Borg
Animal/pet: Cat
Ambitions/goals: To break into journalism, films, television
Clothing store: Flip
Clothing designer: Yohji Yamamoto (big, baggy styles)
Aftershave lotion: Givenchy Gentleman
Fantasy: Winning Wimbledon
Fear: Thatcher winning the next election
Agency: Nev's

It would drive me bananas to wear a suit each day.

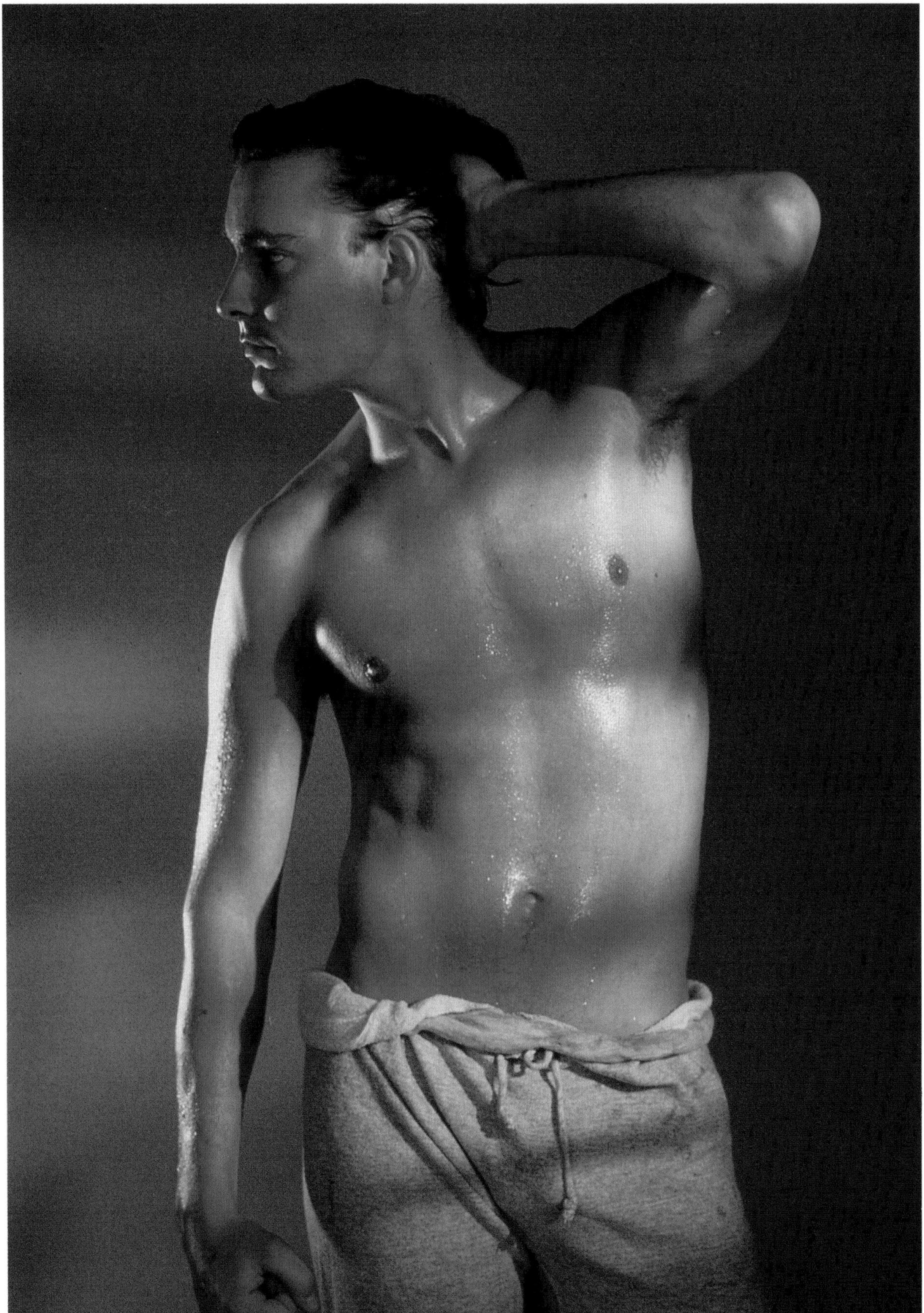

*N*ICHOLAS

*B*ARLEY

*B*orn in Toronto of English parents, Nicholas Barley lived in California for eight years. When he was 9 his family moved to England.

School: When I came to England I went to a public school for a year and then to a comprehensive. The transition between the two schools was horrific – it was like running into a brick wall at 100mph. I went from a fairly sloppy educational system in California to a very strict one and then a very rough one. But I think I emerged all the better for it. I left school with A-levels, then went to work in a bakery.

Modelling: I was in between jobs chopping up fish on the wet-fish counter in Selfridges when my ex-girlfriend, who is a model, suggested I became a model. I had tests done and was accepted quite quickly but carried on with the fish job for about 6 months until they sacked me for having too much time off for modelling.

It took me about two years to find my image, which is long hair. All the female models I work with say they prefer men with long hair, and hair stylists love it – there's so much more you can do with it. I've had a lot of work recently in Paris, Milan, Tokyo and South Africa. Modelling isn't a 9 to 5 job, but when you're

actually working you can work your ass off. You can start at 6 in the morning and go on until 2 the next morning with just a half-hour break. In Tokyo you mainly work weekends.

Time off: If I spent a whole year without going out of London I'd go insane, so I do take holidays. I go all over the place, but always to Capri every year. I also disappear into the country most weekends, to friends with big houses. I love shooting and painting and just walking around the countryside.

Clothes: I mostly wear green combats, bought in the King's Road, whether I'm in London or on a country shoot.

Fitness: I exercise daily, by running five miles round the parks, and I also train at a gym. When I get the opportunity I water-ski and surf. We lived right on the beach in California so I was doing all the stand-up surfing as a young boy. I've also surfed in Bali and South Africa.

Fantasy: If I wasn't a model I would like to be a gamekeeper.

NICHOLAS BARLEY

Birthdate: 25 April 1961
Height: 6'2" (1.88m)
Hair: Fair
Star sign: Taurus
Weight: 13 stones (182lb/ 82.55kg)
Eyes: Blue

Personal favourites
Time of day: Morning
Town: Goudhurst, Kent
Car: E-type Jaguar
Colour: Blue
Food: Meat – in any form
Drink: Milk
Hobbies: Hunting; shooting; painting
Film: *Dr Zhivago*
Actor/actress: Richard Burton
Book: *Death in the Long Grass* (Agatha Christie)
Author: Agatha Christie
Magazine: *Country Life*
TV show: Any wildlife documentary
Hero/heroine: Winston Churchill
Cartoon: Tom & Jerry
Music: All sorts
Musician/group: All sorts
Places to go: Any out-of-the-way country place
Holiday spots: Capri; Bali; California
Sport: Surfing; water-skiing; shooting; cricket
Sportsman/woman: Ian Botham
Animal/pet: Wolfhound
Ambitions/goals: To own a lot of land in the country
Clothing store: Paul Smith
Clothing designer: Paul Smith
Aftershave lotion: Chanel
Fantasy: Having enough money to carry out my ambitions
Agency: Gavin's Models

Picture acknowledgements

Jean Ansado: 82 (right); Henry Arden: 19 (right), 42, 45;
Stefan Bajic: 104; Richard Barnes: 15; Felix Benjamin: 28,
31; Tim Blake: 17; David Bozman: 32 (left), 32-3, 50; Albert
Bray: 81; James Darrell: 68; Andy Earl: 125, 126 (top); Bob
Gothard: 67, 71; Graham Hughes: 43; Clare Hunt: 59; Nick
Jarvis: 56; Les Kingsbury: 19 (left); Serge Krouglikoff: 110;
Trevor Leighton: 127; Virginia Liberatore: 85; Tom
Lowman: 114; Francis Loney: 10, 44, 76-7, 79 (top), 113
(bottom), 123, 124; Mike McGoran: 48-9, 58; Jamie Morgan:
46, Bill Morton: 105, 106; Jan Mostert: 84, 86, 87, 88;
Sanders Nicholson: 54-5; Bob Norris: 57; Toby Piggott-
Brown: 89; Anthony Price: 47; Rico Pultimann: 66, 69, 72-3;
Sabre: 122; Red Saunders: 82 (left); Jeanny Savage: 53; Frits
Schroeder: 116 (top), 117; Elliot Segal: 80; Graham Shearer:
16; Beverley Spanner: 111; Roger Stowell: 51; Mark
Thomas: 11, 12-13, 14; Donna Trope: 29, 30, 32 (top right),
107, 108, 112 (left); Coreen Turner: 113 (top); Ken Yap: 78.

Most photographs have been supplied by the featured
models, and every effort has been made to trace copyright
holders. In the event of any unavoidable omissions in the
above list of credits, rectification will be made in subsequent
editions of the book.